Pickle

The Bitchin' Kitchen and Dinks for All

ISBN: 9798625806114

Harriet Press

Select Publishing House

Incline Village, Summerlin

Thank You

Thank you to my creative husband, Doug, for encouraging me to write this book. We were in COVID-19 lockdown, and I must have been bothering him too much.

A big thank you to John and Pat Sloan who introduced me to this great sport. John also provided many of the candid photos that I used to create the digitized sketches inside, as did Jules Karney. And about the sketches: to those players who were caught doing something right, bravo. To the others who were caught on camera at awkward moments, you know it's in good humor!

Paddles up to all the friends I have made on the courts in Incline Village and Las Vegas. This book is for you. And to the memory of our good friend Tim, the best pickleball player I have ever known.

About Pickleball: The Bitchin' Kitchen and Dinks for All

For the last seven years I have had the time of my life playing pickleball. It has pushed golf and kayaking aside. My new friends, young and old, challenge me to improve while we all laugh and exercise. The gym was never this much fun. I can't wait to share the joy with you.

I'm not the best player in my club, but I'm competitive. My real skill is writing in fun and memorable ways. I have created over 100 popular pickleball newsletters with playing tips. During my forced COVID-19 isolation I decided to turn my ideas into this book.

Players ask where I get my info. I create my tips from good and bad personal experiences and watching others play. Most of my career I observed people and helped them improve on their jobs. Now I'm encouraging others on the courts.

Pickleball is a great equalizer – anyone of any shape, profession, gender or age can play at any skill level and have fun.

Pickleball players fall into the well-known bell curve. The vast majority are social players who have plenty of room to improve skills and keep having fun. This book is for you. A small number of people at one end of the curve will never get better; they are devoid of coordination and focus. I can't help them, but kudos for trying. And I am not qualified to help the small number on the other end of the curve who have outgrown social play and are chasing medals and prize money. They often have addictive tendencies, and they scare me.

Beginners and solid players can cover this book from front to back or pick any page at any time and take in a few paragraphs. There is a lot inside, so you might want to take it in bite-size pieces. Always something to think about. Often a good reminder of something you already know.

I enjoyed writing this and hope I make you smile while you learn a few tricks.

Keep your **paddle up** and remember, it's only a game. But what a game!

Look What's Inside

Why Play Pickleball?

Why take a walk? Ride a bike? Eat a brownie?

There are so many reasons to play pickleball:

It's fun, cheap and gets you off the couch. Better to binge on pickleball than Mad Men.

Pickleball is co-ed and women can beat men. Ha!

It's not tennis. I repeat, it's not tennis!

Spouses and kids can get involved – or not. The family that plays together, well you know.

Meeting new people is always good. I like most of them, though there's always one. . .

It's a sport you can play for a lifetime. I wish I had known about it decades ago.

No reservations needed for drop-in play. No excuses, no lead time, no regrets. Spontaneous and engaging. Play 'til you drop.

Who Plays Pickleball?

Once again, we baby boomers are leading the trend. But we aren't the only ones having fun. Pickleball is growing in school athletic programs. It is a sport you can play from cradle to grave – well almost.

Pickleball is infectious. Not like coronavirus, but in a good way. One person learns to play, loves the game and tells two people, who pass the enthusiasm on to four more people, and so it spreads.

People who are introduced to pickleball while at vacation resorts want to play when they get home. That's what happened to me. So, I pestered our local recreation director to paint some lines on a tennis court and I made a donation to get some portable nets. Where there's an advocate, there's a way. Now we have eight courts and great turnout at daily drop-in play.

So, who plays pickleball? The young and the old; serious athletes, weekend warriors and couch potatoes; golfers and tennis players, walkers and joggers; good guys and bad girls.

Pretty soon, the real question will be: who doesn't play pickleball?

She plays pickleball. He plays pickleball.

And everyone in-between plays pickleball.

All 5'4" of me is on the left.

Where Did it Come From?

Most historians credit the invention of pickleball to Joel Pritchard, a Washington state congressman. Thanks Joel. During the summer of '65 the Pritchard kids were bored, complaining about nothing to do. Taking inspiration from the badminton and tennis courts, they came up with pickleball.

What would you call the game? It's a little like tennis; a bit like ping pong; some aspects of badminton. How about "bad mini tennis pong?"

Lore says the Pritchard family dog kept chasing the ball. The pooch's name was Pickles. I know, but it could have been Pookie or something worse.

Like many things from the 60s, it was forgotten for a while. In 1984 the United States of America Pickleball Association (USAPA) was founded, and the first official rule book was published. The sport had a long, slow fuse but it has exploded in the last decade.

Gearing Up Pickleball Style

It doesn't take much to get started playing pickleball. Players use a hard-surface, short-handled paddle and a whiffle type ball the size of a softball. Most pickleball arenas have paddles beginners can borrow.

The most important gear you need and won't be able to borrow is a pair of court shoes. Some pickleball shoes are on the market now, but they are mostly the same as tennis shoes, maybe with brighter colors. So, find a comfortable pair of tennis shoes.

In pickleball, you will be moving forward, backwards, left and right, often with quick changes of direction. And, you will be jumping and bending. You need a shoe that provides excellent support up to your ankle and can be laced or fastened firmly. Walking or running shoes don't work because they are built to propel you forward. That can lead to injuries during pickleball play, and no one wants to face plant in front of so many fun-loving people. That would be a real downer.

Besides shoes, you'll want sunscreen, sunglasses, a cap or visor. Any clothing that provides freedom of motion will do. There is no need to dress like a country club tennis player. Yes, the tennis folks look good, but pickleball players have more fun!

One more thing that pickleball players always wear – a smile!

Tennis the Menace

Many communities have created multi-purpose courts by adding pickleball lines on tennis courts. With portable nets, four pickleball courts can fit into the area of one enclosed tennis court. That means 16 people can and do play pickleball at one time on one tennis court. Talk about good use of space! And hocus pocus, you'd better learn to focus.

Dedicated pickleball courts are becoming commonplace. And tennis players who previously considered pickleball players to be noisy, annoying, and unfit by tennis standards, are now trying the sport. To their surprise, they find it challenging and fun. Duh. Today there are many crossover players.

Being good at tennis is neither an asset nor a liability for pickleball. Tennis isn't pickleball like soccer isn't football. Tennis players, especially singles players, are usually athletic. But they often have trouble adjusting to the short-handled paddle and the timing of pickleball play. They want to take big backswings instead of blocking shots. And they are more comfortable staying at the baseline than moving forward for the net play.

<u>To all tennis players:</u> welcome to our pickleball courts. Don't tell us what a great tennis player you are. We don't care. Just show us your pickleball stuff, play nice on our courts, and loosen up, we laugh a lot.

The Floor Plan

A pickleball court looks a bit like a scaled down version of a tennis court. There is a net in the middle of the court, a center line marking service sides, and a line between the front and the back sections of each side.

The pickleball net is 36 inches high at the ends and sags to 34 inches in the center.

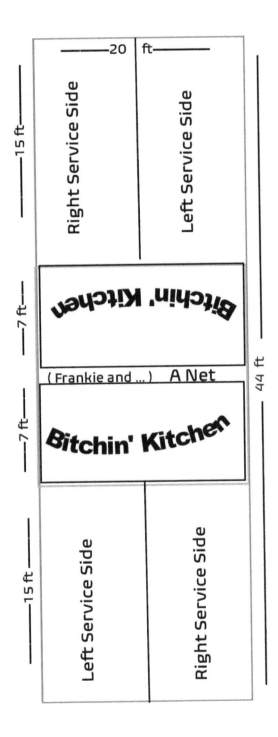

Right Service Side

Left Service Side

20 ft

15 ft

7 ft

Bitchin' Kitchen

(Frankie and ...)   A Net

Bitchin' Kitchen

7 ft

44 ft

Left Service Side

Right Service Side

15 ft

A court is 20 feet wide by 44 feet long, just over half the length of a tennis court. That means each team's half of the pickleball court is only 22 feet long. If you haven't played, you may be thinking pickleball sounds like kid's play.

What makes pickleball so challenging is not the size of the court but the **speed** at which the ball comes back at you, and the fact that it **doesn't bounce** very high. Covering that small court is more difficult than it sounds

There are special rules for the kitchen area. If you are standing in the kitchen, even if you have only one toe on the kitchen line, you **may not hit the ball before it bounces**. If you hit the ball in the air before a bounce, you lose. More about this later.

Game On

Pickleball is most often played as a doubles game. Twice the fun, someone to help you win, someone to blame when your team loses.

The big picture:

One person serves. A player on the other team returns the ball. Tit for tat.

Players keep hitting the ball back and forth across the net until a fault occurs. A fault is a screw up that stops play, like hitting out of bounds or hitting into the net.

A team can score only when they are serving. If the other team messes up, the serving team wins a point and keeps serving.

If the serving team screws up, neither team scores and the serve passes to the next player.

The first team to earn **11 points wins**, provided that is at least 2 points more than the opponents. If the score reaches 11 to 10, the game goes on with the usual rules until one team wins by 2 points, or darkness is called. Most games are completed in about 10 minutes.

Easy peasie, but there are a <u>few more complications:</u>

There is a **two-bounce rule**. The **serve** must bounce once before it is returned, and the **return of serve** must also bounce once. Bounce. Bounce. One bounce per side.

After these first two bounces, a player may return the ball in the air – a volley shot – or may let the ball bounce once before returning it. Your choice every time, after all this is America!

Beware the "kitchen," the front section of the court, 7 feet on each side of the net. If you are standing in the kitchen, you must let the ball bounce. You can't hit the ball on the fly. So, don't stand there and limit your options.

For those who don't know a spatula from a tarantula, staying out of the kitchen is natural. But for others, it doesn't matter how many times we remind players of this rule, someone will violate it during every game. It's just too tempting to swat those higher balls in the air. I've thought about electrifying the kitchen line to make the point, but we don't have power outlets at our courts.

May I Serve You?

You need to get the serve down before you start playing in games.

The serve must be an **underhand movement.** That is one reason you can play pickleball for life. You won't throw out your shoulder trying to smash overhead serves.

Your paddle should connect with the ball **at or below waist high**. That means your waist, not Wilt Chamberlain's. And your paddle head must be **below or level with your wrist** and moving in an **upward arc** when you connect with the ball. Think of the movement like releasing a bowling ball. The arm extension helps direct the placement of your serve. Overhead or sidearm serves are not permitted.

Serving Territory

To serve, when you strike the ball both feet must be behind the baseline and in an area represented by an imaginary extension of the sideline and the middle line of your court.

It's okay if your feet cross the baseline with your follow through <u>after</u> you connect with the ball. One more thing: at least one foot must be on the ground when you connect with the ball – that means no "Air Jordan."

Once you execute the serve correctly from your court – half the battle – it must clear the net and land in the diagonal quadrant of your opponents' court beyond their kitchen line.

If the ball lands in the opponents' kitchen or touches the kitchen line it is short and a fault. If it lands beyond the baseline or outside the center or sideline, you messed up.

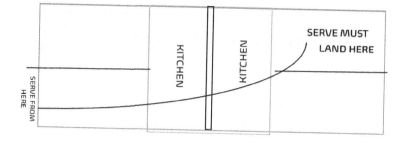

Serving is a Privilege, Make the Most of It

Your team can score points only when serving. Don't blow your serve. There are **no do-overs** unless you hit the top of the net on the way across. If your serve touches the net then somehow lands in the correct section of the opponents' court, it is a **"let"** which means we let you try that again. But, if your serve touches the net and lands in the opponents' kitchen area or out of bounds, you just lost your team's chance to earn a point. Big mistake.

The same player keeps serving as long as his team keeps winning points. The server alternates serving from the right side and the left side of the court. More on the serving rotation later.

If your team loses the serve, you may never get another chance to score. It doesn't usually go that way, but a strong, and lucky, opponent team could rack up 11 points without faulting. Game over. Or as Hillary says, "wha' happened?"

Underhand serve from behind the baseline.

Paddle hits ball below the waist.

Scoring at Pickleball

This isn't about hooking up, although Pickleball is a pretty friendly sport. I'm referring to counting points and announcing scores during a game.

The scoring convention has three numbers, and new players find this confusing. But it's easy as 3-2-1. Me first. The first number is my team's score. The second number is the other guys' score, and the third number says who is serving – the 1st or 2nd server. A score of 3-2-1 means the serving team has 3 points, the receiving team has 2 points, and the server is the number 1 or 1st server for the serving team during this possession.

New players: don't obsess over how to say the correct score until you can actually score some points. It's not the first thing you need to learn.

Different Shots for Different Spots

There are several shots in the game you need to know:

A **dink** is a soft, short shot that goes over the net and lands in your opponents' kitchen. They will have to bend low to return it. A dinking contest is the meat of many points.

A **groundstroke** is a shot you hit after the ball has bounced. A **volley** is a shot you hit before it bounces.

A **passing shot** is like a line drive in baseball. It is an offensive shot that moves fast and in a straight line with no arc. It can be used to keep your opponent away from the net near the back of his court, a good place to stick him.

A **lob** shot travels in a high arc over your opponent's head and lands near her baseline. She will have to turn around to try for it, or just let it go and hope it is long.

An **overhead** shot is one a player reaches high to hit. It is usually hit with a downward stroke and results in a slam the opponent will have trouble returning.

Paddle Pickin'

Once you are addicted to the sport you will want your own paddle - or two. Paddles come in various materials, shapes, weights and colors.

The most important considerations in selecting a paddle are **grip size, weight and color**. Color? Yes, color.

Bright colors make you feel happy and energized. Why not set the mood with a hot pink, orange, or turquoise paddle? Black and dark colors suggest you are a serious player who wants to intimidate the opponents. Yellow paddles give you a slight edge because it is more difficult for the opponents to see the yellow ball coming from your paddle. Some players wear yellow shirts for the same reason. They will do anything to win. But beware: yellow attracts bees so if your courts are surrounded by flowers and fruit trees, you need to be careful.

Once the important decision about color is made, you can move on to the more serious stuff. Beginners, especially those who play tennis, often swing and miss the ball entirely before getting used to the short-handled pickleball paddles. They lament, I need a longer paddle!

USAPA Rules dictate **paddle size**. The width of your paddle plus the length (including the handle) may not exceed 24 inches. A classically shaped paddle is about 8 inches wide by 15-1/2 inches long. If you want a longer paddle, it will have to be narrower or have a very short grip. However, the length may not exceed 17 inches. Still, that gives you some options.

There is no limit on the width of your paddle, but the wider you make it, the shorter it gets. There doesn't seem to be any advantage to that – unless a player has the reach of an adult gorilla and the eyesight of a bat.

Paddles can be any **shape, thickness and weight.** A heavier paddle purportedly gives you more power when hitting the ball, but at the expense of some control. Why would you need more power? You aren't hitting across a football field, just a small pickleball court.

Just a few popular shapes and sizes of paddles.

A paddle that is too heavy for your ability and frequency of play will cause arm or hand strain over time. Tennis elbow has a nice athletic ring to it. But pickleball elbow? That just sounds silly. Yet it can happen if you play with a heavy paddle. Try out different weights. Paddles range from about 6 oz. to 14 oz. You may not notice if you gain an ounce, but you will notice it on your paddle.

Paddles come with and without **edge guards**. Paddles with edge guards probably last longer. But some players prefer a clean surface without the edge.

Paddles may be wood, metal, fiberglass, a composite, any dense, smooth material. The choice of material will affect the overall weight of the paddle.

A **grip** that is too small or too big will also cause you to hold your paddle too tightly. Grips are generally available between 4 and 5 inches, usually in 1/8th inch increments. Grips that are too thick or too slender for your hand can cause hand, wrist and forearm injuries. You can build up a small grip, but you will not be able to slim down a thicker grip.

Paddles that meet the association's standards will say on them: *Approved by USAPA.*

In golf, skiing and so many other sports, it is easy to blame the equipment when you make mistakes. That's because there are so many pieces of gear. In pickleball you have only your paddle, so love yours or leave it and get a new one. An experienced player can play with any paddle, but you want one that gives you confidence and feels comfortable even after several hours of play. A psychological edge is a good thing.

What is the first thing you should do when you acquire a paddle? Put your name on it! Write on the face of the paddle with a permanent marker. Or stick a personalized address label just above the paddle handle. If I had a nickel for every paddle that has been left behind on courts, I would be able to buy a lot of pickles!

Like your sunglasses, your paddle will collect particles and a film of pollutants. Wipe your paddle periodically with a damp cloth and mild dish soap like Dawn. Dry and stow for the next time. If your clean, shiny paddle reflects the sun properly, you could temporarily blind your opponent! One more advantage.

Smile, You're Playing Pickleball

Now that you can serve and you understand the special kitchen rules, it's time to play.

Most pickleball court venues post drop-in play times. No reservations needed, just show up by yourself or with some friends and you will rotate into different games with different players.

Let others know if you are a beginner. They will be gentle with you and most players want to help others. Watch, listen and learn.

If you want to be popular on the pickleball courts, practice **court etiquette.** Players are tolerant, but I do know of a few individuals who have been banned from the courts – voted off the island so to speak. The tribe has spoken.

Follow **local paddle line-up customs** and be ready to play when your turn comes. Play **at your level** when courts are designated by skill. If some better players roll their eyes when you join them, you may be on the wrong court. Your ego is bigger than your get go.

Safety first. If a ball rolls onto your court, stop play. Do not toss the ball onto another court unless someone asks for it. **Stow it, don't throw it.**

Do not use precious table or bench room to stow your backpack, purse, gym bag or jacket. Hang paraphernalia on fencing with a carabiner clip or stow on the ground along fences.

Stay clear of courts when you are waiting for a game. Players need space to serve and reach lobs.

Don't take phone calls during your play. In fact, please mute your phone and leave it in your bag, not in your pocket.

Bring water or a sports drink with you. Drink before, during and after play. No one wants to interrupt drop-in play for a 9-1-1 call. Have a glass now just for practice.

Get ready for the time of your life!

Who's the Proctologist?

Half the enjoyment of pickleball is the people you meet and their preference for fun over form. Drink it in.

Before pickleball it was quite a while since I mixed with such a diverse group of people. Our club (and I use that term loosely) has doctors and patients, a rocket scientist and a trash recycler, bloggers and cloggers and maybe some floggers (they generally don't boast,) a professional shopper, a carpenter and a few studs, bankers and pranksters, teachers and preachers, a black jack dealer and a potato peeler. You get the idea.

Between games you will be hydrating and chit chatting. Learn something about the interesting folks around you while you sip. If you are shy, you'll be starting a conversation with pickleball as a common interest. If you are talkative, you have a ready audience.

Part 2: IN THE GAME

Textbook Pickleball

This is how the pro players do it, or at least how they say they do it.

1. The server executes a deep serve, then stays back with his partner waiting for the return of serve.
2. The receiver hits a deep return after the serve bounces.
3. A player on the serving team waits for the bounce, then hits the next shot soft and short to land in the opponent's kitchen. That's called the 3rd shot drop.
4. All players move to the kitchen line and engage in a dinking rally, adding angles trying to pull an opponent wide. Players keep the ball traveling low over the net, patiently waiting for an opponent to make a mistake. When the opponent hits a ball that is a bit too high, you seize the moment and slam it at his feet or behind her. Good for you.

What's wrong with textbook play? It doesn't consider the real world where someone will always go off script! Learn to expect the unexpected.

Paddle Up

Being ready for anything means keeping your paddle up. Why? Because you won't have time to raise it when a quick volley comes at you.

Many of us think we are keeping our paddle up more often than we actually do. I have taken plenty of candid photos on the courts and I have a hard time finding good examples of players waiting with paddle up.

Next time you play, ask someone on the sidelines to watch you for a few minutes and to tell you how often your paddle isn't in the up and ready position. You might be surprised.

This gal does a great job keeping her paddle up.

Now get up and out of the kitchen!

Having your paddle up means you are alert and ready for anything. It also gives your opponents a target whether they realize it or not. You might be surprised how many shots are unconsciously directed at a raised paddle. It's such a tease.

If you make a habit of placing your other hand on the rim of your paddle when you are ready and waiting, you will find that your paddle is up front more often. Having a second hand on the paddle also helps keep it steady until you are ready to take the shot.

Ready for Anything

When you are in the ready position, you are facing the net with your paddle up and out in front of you. Your weight is evenly distributed and on the balls of your feet, so your heels barely touch the ground. I should be able to insert a love note under the back of your shoe without you even realizing it. And those knees are bent slightly.

Bent knees and weight on the front of your feet help you spring into action when you need to move up or shuffle sideways.

23

Paddle up and out in front, weight evenly distributed, knees slightly bent; she is ready for anything the opponents send her way.

From the ready position you can quickly rotate your paddle face to block a shot, reach up or extend your arm sideways, bend low to pick up a shot near your feet, or pivot to change the angle of your shot. It will be difficult for the opponents to get past you.

Eye on the Ball Says it All

You may think it's just a whiffle ball, but those yellow rounds meet very specific requirements. The rules dictate the size and weight with only narrow variances. The ball must be molded from a durable material without any texture. The ball must fall within a hardness range measured on a Durometer D scale and must bounce 30 to 34 inches when dropped from a height of 78 inches onto a granite surface plate at ambient temperature of 75 to 80 degrees. (I'm not making this up!)

And those holes. There must be between 26 and 40 of them, spaced appropriately. The bigger the holes, the fewer there will be. The balls with the larger holes are customarily used for indoor play but any approved ball is acceptable for indoor or outdoor play.

A good player will be able to adjust his game slightly based on the ball being used. When you can tell if you are playing with a harder ball or a softer ball, you are no longer a rookie. Congratulations.

Now that you know all about those balls, take a close look. Really. **Watch the ball come all the way to your paddle.** Focus on seeing the holes even if it makes you cross-eyed. Watch the ball hit your opponent's paddle and come off it toward you. A sure way to swing and miss is to take your eye off the ball. Besides inviting an error, taking your eye off the ball to look where you want to aim it signals to your opponents where they should expect the return shot. Don't give them that edge. Always watch the ball.

If you aren't watching the ball meet your paddle, you are counting on reflex and luck. Reflexes tire, and luck runs out.

Don't Clock It, Just Block It

Many players enjoy the feel of hitting the ball hard. Come on, admit it. We wind up to get momentum for a big slam. This is especially true of tennis players who are used to a long-handled racquet and the longer distance from baseline to baseline.

In pickleball there just isn't time to take a backswing. The ball comes at you so much faster and the court isn't that big. If you want to control your return, you must learn to simply punch or block a shot, especially when you are near the kitchen zone playing the short game.

With our hard-surfaced paddles and balls, your return shot can go far with little effort. If you hold your paddle in front of you to fend off a fast-incoming shot, your return could reach near the opponents' baseline with no backswing at all.

In addition, it is most effective to take your pickleball shots with your paddle in front of you. When you let the ball get to your side or behind, you lose control. But you can't hit in front of your body when you are wasting time taking a backswing.

When you are in the ready position, your paddle is in front of you. Open or close the face of your paddle slightly to set the angle. Extend your arm from the elbow joint, keeping your wrist firm, to punch at the ball. Make contact with the ball as far out front of your body as possible for more control. Don't let the paddle drop below your wrist. And remember to bend your knees!

Court Prime Real Estate

We know where the kitchen is on the pickleball courts—there's a line defining it. Just as in an active home, the kitchen is the meeting place. It's where all the action is. Good things happen around the kitchen. You want to get to the kitchen line to score.

The kitchen line is like lakefront property: it's prime real estate. The baseline is like a low rent apartment; it's where you start out when you aspire to move up.

When you are at the baseline, you are on the defense. It's difficult to place a winning shot from there, and your opponents have more time to react to your shot. You might find yourself alone if you hang around the baseline while the other players get to the kitchen. You aren't helping your partner if you stay back.

The section of the pickleball court halfway between the kitchen line and the baseline is simply a place to pass through. Nothing good happens there. It has neither the allure of the lakefront homes nor the convenience or familiarity of the condo. You don't want to stop there. If you get jammed mid-court by a skilled opponent, defend yourself as best you can, then get up to the kitchen asap.

Movin' On Up

For best control, you want to return the ball with your paddle out in front of you, feet firmly planted at the time you connect. This is a pretty natural position when you are at the kitchen line. But getting there has its risks.

Moving forward from the baseline to the kitchen line means you must pass through "no man's land," the least desirable part of the court. When you are stuck there, bad things can happen. Your opponents have an easy target at your feet. They can hit toward you when you are still moving. If you hesitate because the ball is too short to reach as a volley, it may drop at your side just behind you. That's a very difficult shot to return and you'll wish you had somehow taken it in the air.

So, even in awkward places and poor positions, plant your feet as soon as the ball leaves your opponent's paddle and do your best to take the ball in front of you whenever possible. Then keep on movin' up.

The Pickleball Dance

This isn't about the little victory jig some of us do when we deliver a good shot. This is about the way you should move on the court all the time.

Think of the pickleball court as the dance floor, practice and master the **1-2-3 Step**.

1 - Start behind the baseline to serve, one foot forward and one foot slightly back. 2- Move your back foot forward to balance your stance behind the baseline waiting for your opponent's return of serve. 3 - Boogie up to the kitchen line, waiting in the ready position. That's the Pickleball 1-2-3 Step. Only wall flowers stay at the baseline.

At the kitchen, you begin a **line dance**. Stay abreast with your partner, shuffling right and left together when the opponents give you a wide shot. Paddle up, light on your feet, weight on your toes not your heels.

Now that you've got the rhythm, your dance card will be full. **Everyone likes a partner who can move.**

These players can hear the music! But this isn't what I meant! Maybe I overdid the dance analogy.

Move with your partner, not to your own tune.

The Serve is Important, But it's No Big Deal

The serve is important because your team can't win if your serve isn't in. A team has an opportunity to score points only when they are serving. You blow your serve you miss your chance. That ship has sailed. Your opponents could be sleeping or comatose and you still lose to them. Now that would be embarrassing!

Unlike tennis, no one keeps statistics on ace serves in pickleball. The serve is simply a way to start a rally. Your obligation is to land a safe serve, stay back for the return of serve, then let the serious play begin. The third shot of the rally generally gets the real action going. So, serve it tame to start the game.

Some players don't accept this and work on backhanded and spin serving techniques. Those variations tend to be low percentage winners and risk losing the chance to score a point. I wouldn't waste time on perfecting a killer serve when **other skills will pay off more often**. If you watch videos of pro pickleball players, you see that many gold medalists have pretty tame serves. In golf, the longer you make your backswing on the tee box, the more can go wrong. In pickleball, the more you try to crank up your service motion, the more can go wrong.

If you want to make more of your serve, practice changing it up – deep, then occasionally soft and shorter; low, then throw in a lob serve; to the receiver's forehand, forehand, then backhand. The change up adds challenge without the risks of faulting with spin or backhand serves.

Scoring and Serving Protocol

The 3-digit score must be called before the serve begins each time.

Position and score work like this: whoever is standing on the right side of either partnership when a new game begins, will always be on the right side of the court when the team's score ends with an even number, 0, 2, 4 etc. That's a hint to figure out where you should be.

Sometimes you change places with your partner while chasing a ball during a point. When play stops, you need to get back into the correct place for the next serve.

Don't fret the small stuff, your partner will help you get where you ought to be.

Serving Rotation - I'm Number One

The serving rotation works this way: only one player on the **first team to serve in a new game** gets to serve. She keeps going until her team makes an error. Then the serve passes to the opponents. That's called a **side out**.

After that first side out, each player on each team gets a shot at serving during the team's possession before the serve goes back to the other team. That means each team gets two chances to screw up before the other team gets its chance to serve and score.

If you are standing on the right side of the court when your team gets the serve, then you are server #1 **for that service round only**. If your partner happens to be on the right side the next time your team starts serving, then she is #1 and you just dropped down to #2. No one stays #1 forever. It's situational.

Who Should Serve First for Your Team?

At the beginning of each game, each team gets in position on their side of the court with one player on the right side of the court. That is the person who will serve first for that team. So, does it matter which one of you serves first?

Maybe. No one player stays in the serving position for long, but there can be some strategy in deciding who should start.

Assuming both players are right-handed and can land a safe serve, the less dominant player may wish to start as server. That's because a player on the left side is responsible for covering a greater portion of the court with a forehand shot. The player on the right is responsible for landing the serve and covering the right-side alley.

If one partner is struggling to land good serves, the more reliable server may want to go first and try to chalk up some points for a head start. It's a confidence builder that gets your team's momentum going.

If your team has one leftie and one right-handed player, the leftie serves first so the team starts with the strength of two forehands covering the middle of the court, the hot spot for activity.

Better Return that Serve

Like the serve, the return of serve is a preliminary part of each rally. It's the second step leading to the third shot and the crux of the game.

Keeping the return of serve in play is just as important as landing a safe serve. Maybe more important. If you mess up your serve, you lose a chance to score but no one gets a point. If you mess up your return of serve, the other guys get one point closer to eleven. Ouch, that hurts.

That should tell you this is no time to go for a winner or try something tricky. Your job is simply to land a safe return, the deeper the better to keep your opponents in the back court on the defense.

Your Partner is Receiving so Where are You?

The receiver's partner is permitted to stand anywhere on or off the court. So, where do you choose to be?

You won't have to wait for the next ball to bounce because the serve and the return will be the first two bounces. So, you can choose to stand at the kitchen line. Your job is to watch the served ball land and call any short, long or wide faults so your partner, the receiver, can concentrate on returning the shot. Unless you have eyes in the back of your head, you should stand at a slight angle for a full view of your partner's side of the court.

Stand out of your partner's way so she can make a cross court return if desired. Some players stand so far aside they are barely on the court. That's a bit dramatic and unnecessary. Yes, it gives your partner a wide clearance to hit, but it also gives the serving team a wide area to land their next shot.

If you stand closer to the center line, you can become an annoying presence that forces the opponent server to target a much narrower landing area. Crowding the center line can be a good place to start. However, once the served ball is on its way, you should shuffle away from the center to give your partner room.

B.F.F.N.

When you join drop-in pickleball play groups, you meet new people who become very important to you. They may not become your BFF (best friend forever) but everyone you partner with during a game will be your BFFN (best friend for now.)

What do BFFs do? They talk to you often, they have your back, they support you regardless, and they celebrate your wins. Silent partners may be good in business, and sometimes in marriage, but they do not make good pickleball partners.

Chatter can matter. I had the pleasure of playing with a much better partner recently. Together we were awesome. What made it work is that my partner talked to me throughout the game. I knew exactly where she was at all times, and what was expected of me. We didn't get in each other's way, and we didn't let balls pass between us because each thought the other would take it.

Communication between partners helps avoid unforced errors that come when you expect something from your partner, and he doesn't deliver it. The best partners move as a single force, together at the baseline, together at the net, together in their strategy.

"Yours" and **"mine"** are the most important words you can exchange, especially with new partners. Get used to it by trying to call every shot. Even if you agree in advance that the partner with the forehand will take the shots in the middle, you can still call them.

"**Bounce it**" should also be used frequently. This means you think the ball may be out and you are alerting your partner not to hit it until you see where it lands.

When you are not side by side with your partner, give directional clues. Tell him to move up, or to go back when necessary. Shout "**switch**" when you are behind your partner and want her to cross to the other side.

Check in with your partner if you miss a shot. Ask, did you have it? Yes or no, you will learn from a mistake.

Complimenting good shots and shaking off errors also help pump up a partner and make a stronger team.

She's ready to catch a baseball. He's ice skating. They need to communicate the game is pickleball!

Why doesn't everyone share partner chatter? Maybe we think it is being bossy to call shots. Maybe we expect the other person to read our minds. Talk is a great bargain; **it's cheap, yet very valuable.** Get in the habit of communicating frequently. Eventually, sharing important information will become natural.

Keep Your Partner Near Your Heart

The strength of a partnership is the formidable barrier you create when you are abreast and at the kitchen line. If you are both at the kitchen line and reach your arms out from your sides, you will see you have the whole court covered. Your opponents will have a hard time hitting through you. They might resort to a lob shot, but that's a difficult shot to execute consistently on our short courts.

The **worst position** you can assume as partners is **one player standing forward, the other at the baseline.** This leaves a major section of the court unattended. Your skilled opponents will easily place a shot behind the forward player where neither of you can reach it. You might as well be playing singles.

If you have a partner who rarely moves forward despite your coaxing or badgering, you are better off joining him at the baseline than separating with one player front and one player back. Two wrongs don't make a right, but side by side creates a better defensive barrier than front and back, even if you are deeper in the court.

Partners that move together, groove together. When one partner sidesteps left, so does his dance partner. When one player is pulled back, so goes the other. These moves should be smooth like a tide rolling in and out. You want to see your partner out of the corner of your eye most of the time. So, <u>never be too far apart, keep your partner near your heart.</u>

Perfectly in sync, moving forward after hitting the 3rd shot.

These players are mirror images, right and left-handed.

Lefties – The Odd Fellows

You are in the groove, playing pretty well and syncing with your partner of the moment. Suddenly everything gets thrown off because one of your opponents, or maybe your new partner, is left-handed. He's one of only 10% of the U.S. population.

Have you ever noticed how left-handers are often grumpy because they face challenges every day that the rest of us don't even notice? The world is built for right-handed folks. But that gives left-handers an advantage. They have learned to be very **adaptable**.

Experienced players know the importance of hitting to weak backhands and avoiding feeding shots to strong forehands. But you can't play smart if you don't even notice that one opponent is left-handed. Start each game by checking the paddle hand of the other players.

When one opponent is a lefty, there will be times when both of your opponents' forehands are in the middle. Your typical shot down the center will be feeding balls to their strength. Don't do it. You'll need to change strategy.

When your opponents win a point, they must switch places and now their backhands are both in the center. Great time to go back to the middle shots. You need to think through each shot and adjust accordingly. A good lefty opponent will keep you on your toes.

A lefty will have a different cross court angle and will be in position to hit down the alley on the side you aren't expecting. Those serves you've been practicing to land at the baseline + center line intersection, forcing a backhand return from your opponent, will now approach a lefty on his forehand. Think it through.

If the lefty is your partner, you should agree at the beginning of the game which player will try to take the center shots. Two forehands in the middle or two backhands in the middle each create their own problems. It is more important than ever to communicate and calling every ball will avoid confusion.

Your Better Half

What should you do when your partner is a better player than you are? Hey, it could happen!

Be thankful for a lucky draw, your partner will carry you. But stay alert. When the opponents figure out that you are the weaker player, you will be targeted.

Let your partner take the ball as often as she is in position to do so. Stay out of the way. Talk to each other. Don't surprise your partner. If you feel you have the shot, call it.

Move with your partner, staying abreast and sidling left and right. Let him know where you are at all times. When you call a shot, **just keep the ball in play**. Trying too hard will lead to unforced errors.

Accept that poaching may be part of your team's strategy. Don't be offended if your skilled partner crosses in front of you to put away a shot, or two. It's a smart move, so just take one for the team.

At the end of the game, thank your accomplished partner and ask for one tip to improve your play. You may get something useful or not, either way he will appreciate that you are interested in improving.

High or Low, Which Way to Go?

Would you rather reach up to return a ball, or bend down to get it? Yep, me too. It is much easier to reach up. It feels good to stretch. And you can jump to extend your reach. The sky's the limit.

Bending to reach a low shot is more difficult. It's harder on the knees and the back if not executed properly. The ground gets in the way. And looking down exaggerates your double chins.

Bending changes your center of gravity. More falls occur from players bending low than reaching high. And you can't do much with the low shot if you get it. You must hit up on the ball to clear the net, but not so high that you send a juicy meatball to your opponents. This requires skill and practice.

If it's harder for <u>you</u> to return a ball at your feet, then it is also more difficult for your opponents. **That's your money shot.** Aim for the feet whether your opponent is at the baseline or at the kitchen line. It's especially effective to hit at the feet while those feet are moving forward. That is one of the most difficult pickleball shots to return. If you master hitting at the feet on your opponent's backhand side, you can take that shot to the bank. So <u>hit at the feet, and you will defeat</u>!

Bend at the Knees, Please

A new pickleball doesn't bounce very high. The gently used balls we usually play with have lost some of their resilience and bounce even lower. If you want to play lifetime pickleball, you must use your knees to bend for the low balls. Bending at the waist will eventually strain your back. It also changes your center of gravity, putting you at risk for a fall.

Bending helps you lift a low ball to clear the net. If you don't bend, or if you bend just slightly at the waist, you are more likely to hit the ball into the net. Can you bend with your knees low enough to see the tape on the top of the net at your eye level?

He's got it going on! Great knee bend and balance, paddle out front lifting the dink up and over the net.

Good eye protection too. He could be a pickleball poster boy!

Bend with your knees to save your back, maintain the center of gravity in your core area, and have a better chance of executing the slight upward trajectory needed to clear the net.

Follow Through is Like Your Steering Wheel

You can envision where you want the ball to go, but sometimes it seems to have a mind of its own. The best way to make the ball go where you want is to follow through on your stroke.

Keep your eye on the ball as it hits your paddle, then push through with your arm extended pointing in the direction you want the ball to go.

44

Point where you want the ball to land.

That's great follow through.

Hit In-Between, Split the Team

Shots you return to the center of your opponents' court add confusion to their partnership. Who is going to take the shot?

The most enthusiastic player will want it. The forehand player should take it. The stronger player will try to get it. Both players will collide while trying to make the shot. Or each player will think the other one has it and no one gets it. So many things can go wrong. Those are great reasons to aim between the opponents.

Two good players, one forehand, one backhand. The ball is almost there. Will one of them back off?

There are two more reasons to place your shots between your opponents. The net is shorter in the middle than at the posts, so returning a ball across the center third of the net is a bit more forgiving for low shots.

Also, it is more difficult for your opponents to hit a winning sharp-angled shot from the center area. Center shots are usually returned as straight shots, easier for you to handle.

Hitting in-between players isn't necessarily hitting to the center line. The center line on the court has only one purpose: to identify the serving and receiving quadrants. Once the serve has been executed, the center line is meaningless and should disappear from your mind. Hitting down the center means hitting between the two opponents wherever they have positioned themselves at any given time.

Your opponents will figure out the value of hitting between you and your partner as well. The best defense is to communicate; decide at the start of a game who should take most of the middle shots and call the shots that are close.

Living Targets are Fair Game

On a small pickleball court, two opponents near the net across from you seem like pretty big targets. There are times when you will accidently hit a ball right at an opponent's body. There are also times when you will take aim at the other guy because if you hit him, you win.

It isn't poor sportsmanship to hit at an opponent, though it may be crossing the line if you pummel a beginner or an older, slow-moving target. And deliberately hitting above the chest is just plain nasty and risky.

Getting hit may sting a little, and many players feature red and purple pickleball bruises. But taking a hit in good humor is the best response. And remember to wear that eye protection.

If you want to be invited back to play, just take **aim at your opponent's toes, not his nose.** It's easier to make friends that way. And, it is a very effective play.

Don't Let the Ball Get Too Close

If a ball in play hits you before it bounces on your court, it is a fault against you.

If a ball bounces anywhere on the court and then hits you, it is a fault against you.

If a ball is speeding high out of bounds and it hits you even when you are standing all the way to the fence, it is a fault against you.

If your partner's return of serve hits you, it is a fault against you.

If your opponent's ball hits you because you are a big, scary presence at the kitchen line, it is a fault against you.

If a ball bounces off your paddle and hits you, you just gave yourself a fault.

If you catch a ball in play, even if you are standing out of bounds, it is like being hit and a fault against you.

In other words, getting hit by a ball is always your fault. So, **duck, swivel or jump to avoid being hit.**

Antz in Your Pantz

Have you noticed how some good players seem antsy while they are waiting for you to serve? They never stand still.

A body in motion tends to stay in motion, while a stationary body needs a boost to get going. Thank you, Sir Isaac Newton.

In pickleball, you must be quick on your feet. Staying in motion gives you a head start. Shuffle your feet a bit while waiting for someone to serve. When you are planted in the ready position, roll onto your toes, keep your feet flexible, and you will be ready to make a quick move. Every second counts.

Anticipation - You Git What You Hit

Every action has a reaction. The ball comes back quickly in pickleball so the better you can anticipate it the better you will be prepared to respond.

Playing the odds is something we do in Nevada. It works in pickleball too. Many of the shots you hit come back at you the same way you sent them.

When you hit a hard driving shot, chances are you get a hard return. When you hit a soft shot, you likely get a soft shot back. Hit a tight angle, and if it comes back, it will probably be as a mirrored angle shot. A high lob often brings on a high lob return. Why is that? Well, some of this is just basic geometry. Also, it takes a pretty skilled player to change the pace and direction on shots. So, when you are trying to anticipate your opponents' shots, remember that often <u>you git what you hit.</u>

The Two-Inch Advantage

Two inches doesn't sound like much. But, would you like your waist to be 2 inches smaller? If your hair grew 2 inches, would you need a haircut?

The pickleball net is 34 inches high in the center and 36 inches high at the ends. That 2-inch difference could save your shot.

The 2-inch advantage is especially important when you are dinking the ball from below the net, or while making a valiant effort to reach a short, wide shot your talented opponents delivered. Don't go for the higher hurdle at the sidelines, just aim across the center of the net. When you are back in position and your opponent's drop shot is a bit higher you can go for the alley shot.

Cute Angles

Or is that acute angles? Angled shots are beautiful to watch. In fact, that's exactly what happens. Often the opponents are not prepared for a short angle from you and all they can do is watch it and applaud your skill. If a light-footed opponent manages to reach the shot, you will have a wide-open court to return his valiant save for your ultimate winner.

When passing shots – like line drives in baseball - keep coming back at you, good players incorporate short angled shots into their strategy. The angles pull your opponents out of position, giving you **open spaces for winning places**. Use your leading shoulder and pivot your feet slightly to execute the angled shot.

If you are on the receiving end of a short, angled shot and you manage to reach it, do your best to get back into place immediately. It isn't easy but staying off court is futile. A good partner will move sideways to help cover some of the open space you create.

Play it Smart, Hit Where They Aren't

Since hitting a ball while you are moving is more difficult to control, what does this say about your offensive game? You should hit the ball toward a place that requires your opponent to move.

If the other guy must return your shot while he is on the move, he will lose some control of placement and pace. If he is back, hit short. If he is near the center, hit down an alley. If he is up front, hit behind him. Make him move for the extra challenge and separate him from his partner.

The Money Shots

Do you know the money shots in pickleball? High percentage shots are those that you are likely to win, or that set you up for a winning shot. Use them often.

The high percentage shots are:

1. A passing shot down the middle between your opponents.
2. A soft drop shot into the middle of your opponents' kitchen area.
3. A shot at your opponents' feet anywhere on the court, but especially when they are approaching the kitchen line.
4. A shot to your opponent's backhand.

On the other hand, the lob is a sucker shot. It may work occasionally, but it is risky, and the odds of success go down as the speed of the wind, or the height of your opponent goes up. A lob shot is generally used as a last resort when you get into trouble. If it works, it buys you time to regroup.

Recognizing Defense v. Offense

At times your team will be put on the defense during play. At other times you can play offensively. Knowing the difference helps you avoid low percentage shots.

We all know by now that partners together at the kitchen line form the strongest offensive team. They are positioned to hit dinks, short angles, slams at the opponents' feet, and strategic lobs.

Sometimes you may have trouble getting to the kitchen because the opponents are drilling hard deep shots at you. You are completely defensive at this point. Your only goal is to **keep the ball in play** while looking for an opening to move forward. This is not a time to attempt winning shots. When you are at the baseline, you are not in position to execute high percentage winners like short angles.

When you are being kept back on the defense, try to hit softer, shorter shots to your opponents, shots they will need to let bounce before returning. As they wait for the bounce, you have bought some time to move forward. It's only a few seconds, but it can make all the difference in the game.

What's good for the goose is bad for the gander. Reverse these tips to keep your opponents on the defense. Don't give them openings to come to their kitchen line.

Different Place, Different Pace

What's the best thing about being unpredictable? You keep the other guys off guard.

For those times when you get beyond the first three shots in a rally, take advantage of opportunities to change your target. Hitting several shots in a row to the opponent directly across from you turns his partner into an idle "spectator," one likely to relax his guard. Maybe he drops his paddle or lets his attention stray.

So, a sudden change of direction hitting at the idle spectator is a high percentage shot.

Same with change of pace. Follow several hard hits with a soft shot. This is more difficult to do but when you master it, you will become the master. Turning a soft shot into a screamer is easier _if_ you wait for the right opportunity such as a short shot that comes to you a foot above the net.

The Lob: Love It or Lose It

The lob has its place in your game, but it isn't a shot most players count on. The pickleball court is just too short. Executing a lob makes sense when your opponents are at the kitchen line, or if they are little people. When opponents are up front, there are less than 15 feet of court space behind them. To lob, you need to execute a shot that is high enough to escape the opponents' reach, but with an arc that will have the ball hit the ground before it goes past the baseline. No easy feat.

If you and/or your partner are at the baseline trying to move forward, hitting a lob shot can buy you time. Your opponents need to move back to make any attempt at returning the lob. It takes a second for the lob and the opponent to get there. Only a second or so, but that can make a difference in your positioning. That is the most valuable aspect of the lob. It's like a rescue shot in golf; it gets you out of trouble and back in the point.

If your opponent can return your lob, it is likely to be with a lob or a weak deep shot. Nothing you can't handle.

Beware attempting lob shots when your opponents are mid-court. If they are smart, they will let it go. If they aren't smart, they may jump up to hit your shot that probably would have gone out, giving you another chance to score. But counting on your opponents' errors is not the best strategy.

Incoming Lob: Duck or Cover

When you are at the kitchen line and your opponent hits a lob over your head, how do you respond?

If you see your partner by your side at the kitchen line, one of you may choose to make a run for it. Backing up, especially while looking up, is dangerous and leads to falls. Instead, make a U-turn and move to the back, perhaps in time to attempt a blind return shot. Most often, we just let it go and hope it lands out. Executing an effective lob on short pickleball courts is difficult and a pretty low percentage shot, so don't obsess if your opponents get one now and then.

If you do not see your partner by your side, she may be moving into position behind you to get the shot. So, help your partner by ducking immediately, giving her a full court to work with.

If you have a good partner who was able to move from his spot across the back to get the lob behind you, he will yell "switch" which is your cue to stay at the kitchen line but quickly sidestep to cover the side of the court he just vacated.

So, duck to get out of the way, or move to cover the other side of the court if your partner commands.

It's Your Job

Every player has a job to do, and it varies depending where you are in the game.

When you serve, land a safe serve and stay behind the baseline to await the return of serve. Don't creep up too early.

When your partner serves, stay behind the baseline to await the bounce on the opponent's return of serve.

When you are receiving a serve, stand back far enough for a deep serve. It's easier to move forward than backward.

When your partner is receiving serve, stand ready at the kitchen line but look behind you to watch the serve land. Be ready to call a fault if there is one. Watch for a let serve or one that lands in the kitchen.

When your partner moves, you move in the same direction – up, back, left or right. Try to stay together to provide the best defensive line.

When you are in a rally, just keep the ball in play until the other guy makes a mistake, or until you or your partner gets a chance to place or slam a winner.

When your partner is bigger or fiercer than you, just keep the ball in play until she has a chance to put it away.

No-Brainers

You should be doing these things automatically without ever needing to think about them. Use your brain for more complex moves like hitting perfect placements and disguise shots. When these moves become automatic, you are ready for some of the finer points of the game.

Hold your paddle up.

Bend your knees and keep a spring in your feet.

Keep your eye on the ball all the way to your paddle.

Stay back for return of serve.

Move with your partner and get to the net.

Get out of the kitchen after you return a dink.

Hydrate between games.

PART 3: THE NEXT LEVEL OF PLAY

Squaring Up - Let's Face It

Beginners learn how to assume the ready position: face the net, feet shoulder width apart, weight balanced evenly, knees slightly bent, paddle up and out in front. That works pretty well. But for better positioning, instead of facing the net squarely learn to **face the opponent who has the ball**. It's only a slight adjustment, but it gives you an advantage in reaching and executing your backhand or forehand shots smoothly.

Making small adjustments to square up to whichever opponent has the ball during a rally also keeps your feet moving and helps you concentrate on tracking the ball with your eyes. It's a small thing, but great players are formed from the sum of many small skills and smart advantages.

Backhands - Learn to Turn

When I stand facing the net with the paddle in my hand and my arm fully stretched to the side for a forehand shot, I can reach about 36 inches from my body. That's more than half my height. When I move my arm across my body to make a backhand shot, I can reach only about 24 inches from my body. No wonder those pesky backhand shots are so difficult.

The best way to extend your backhand reach is to turn your body 90 degrees, facing the sideline instead of the net. It's easy. Just move one leg and pivot to gain 50% more reach.

Returning a backhand while standing facing the sideline instead of the net gives you room for a full swing and follow through when you need it. Doesn't matter your size or body shape, <u>when you learn to turn, backhands are no concern.</u>

Feet face the sideline for a clean backhand stroke. Hope he let it bounce: one foot is in the kitchen!

Stay in the Momentum

In general, most of us agree that we should let the player who has the forehand shot take those balls that come between two players.

But there is a lot to be said for momentum and being in the action. If you are engaged in a dinking rally, a good opponent will return the dink further from you each time, pulling you to one side. Your partner will be watching and sidestepping back and forth with you. Even if the ball gets closer to your partner and his forehand, you might want to keep control because you are "in the moment." Your adrenaline is pumping, your eyes are alert, and your feet are light. You've got this. But sometimes an impatient partner will want in on the action and go for the shot prematurely. That often leads to a team mistake.

Same applies to a volley battle across the net. Let the player who is in the moment keep control until it is clear the shot is out of her reach. Once again, calling your shots really pays off.

Hell No, Let it Go

When you are between games and watching others play, you surely notice that many of us hit a lot of balls that would have been out. Not a game goes by when you don't hear someone thanking the opponents for the "gift."

The pickleball court is pretty small, so it is common for players to hit balls that are long and out of bounds. Or at least they would be out of bounds if we learned to let them go. But so many of us love to return a juicy high ball. Like a high pitch in baseball, it's a **sucker shot**. Hitting a ball that would have gone out is giving away a sure thing in exchange for only a 50/50 chance at getting that same thing back, nothing extra. Why would you do that? You might mess up on the return. Even if you don't, it isn't likely you will hit a winner when you have to reach high for the ball. All you are doing is letting your opponents back into the point, and anything can happen. Learning when to let it go can make a huge difference in your wins.

Self-control involves being aware of where you are on the court, and whether the wind is a factor. How hard did your opponent hit the ball? If you are at the kitchen, there are less than 15 feet behind you. If a ball is coming fast and above your shoulders, there is a good chance it will be long. If you are mid-court, please don't jump up to hit a high ball. It will surely go past the baseline if you just let it go.

This guy can jump, but geez, he's near the baseline. Let it go!

Play attention to these clues. When an opponent reaches high to return a ball. she is more likely to hit it longer than a player who bends to return a low shot. Balls that bounce before your opponent hits are less likely to be long than balls that are hit in the air. Taller opponents tend to hit more long balls.

The best aid to help you hold back is a talkative partner, one who yells "no" or "bounce it" early and often. Sometimes the warning comes too late and you can't stop your movement. With practice you will find a way to pull back when you need to.

Real Men – and Women - Dink

It may be hard to accept, but if you watch tournament videos you will see that dinking dominates most matches. Patient pro players have long dinking rallies until someone makes a mistake. **Don't think, just dink**. That makes pickleball more a game of skill than thrill. It's like golf where hackers love to show off their strength from the tees with their drives, but the champions have short game skills and one putts. Driving for show, putting for dough. <u>Slamming for thrill, dinking for skill</u>.

When you learn to initiate dinking rallies, you disarm strong hitting opponents and equalize the game. Players of any size, strength, and skill level can dink. It's easy to practice. Flexibility and patience dominate. Use your knees to get low and open your paddle face to lift the ball over the net. Wait for the other guy to make a mistake.

Jeepers Creepers

Most points are won at the kitchen line. But that doesn't mean you should rush to get there when your team is serving. Remember that you must let the return of serve bounce before the short volleys begin.

Are you a creeper? I know I am. I stand well behind the baseline to serve, then I take a few steps forward as I watch my serve land perfectly in the opponent's court. But those few steps place me too far forward and out of line with my partner. My skilled opponent returns a deep shot and it reaches my feet with little room for me to get my paddle on it. I'm screwed.

I know I'm not alone trying to break this bad habit. So, I appreciate any of you who partner with me reminding me to stay back until we receive the return of serve. I'll do the same for you.

Poaching, It's Not Just for Eggs

Do you ever feel like you and your partner are scrambling and getting nowhere? The score shows you are fried. Maybe you should try poaching. This is especially effective if you have a hard-boiled baseline partner who doesn't like to come to the kitchen line.

Poaching is when the forward player moves across the court to cut off a shot heading toward his partner. It can be a surprise tactic against opponents. It is often used by strong players who become impatient when the opponents are pummeling their weaker partner. Done right, poaching is very effective. But done too often, it becomes predictable.

If you do poach, you must hit a winner. If you don't, your side of the court is wide open for your opponents to score. And your partner will be justified in saying your partnership is toast.

Wait to Celebrate

How many times have you hit a great shot and counted the point in your head, knowing the opponent will never get to it? You relax your attention, then to your surprise the ball somehow comes back over the net and the other team wins the rally.

The game doesn't stop just because you deserve applause for your terrific shot. Remember that a shot isn't a great shot until the opponent faults. So, get back into position, paddle up, eyes on the ball, prepared to play just in case your opponent gets lucky with a return. There is enough time to celebrate after the ball is dead.

Counting another team out because you have a big lead is also premature. Many a partnership has rallied from a significant deficit to win the prize and leave their opponents wondering what went wrong.

Who is that Masked Man?

Hopefully the era of wearing personal protective masks will be behind us when you read this book. Whether they are disguised or not, we need to size up the other players before each game.

Start with your partner. If you've seen her before, consider what you know about the way she plays. Does she move to the kitchen quickly or stay back? Is she aggressive about taking shots? A banger or a dinker? How do your games mesh? You will need to think about your strengths as a team.

If your partner is unfamiliar to you, ask a few questions like: what's your favorite shot? How's your backhand? Any injuries? This might help set expectations about what you can count on.

Now consider the opponents. If you know they are powerful, keep dinking and low shots on the top of your strategic plays. You want to slow them down and change the game. If they look like giants, forget lobbing. Are they a couple? Maybe you can get them to squabble by hitting shots down the middle.

Sizing up the competition keeps you alert to your own strategic advantages.

Recipe for the Kitchen

It's pretty simple, but I frequently hear incorrect information about the kitchen rules during discussions. Players think they may not enter the kitchen until the ball bounces. Not so.

There is **no penalty for standing in the kitchen**. Really. Hang out all day if you wish. But just because something is legal, doesn't make it smart. Being in the kitchen is like trying to box with your hands tied behind you. It's a dumb place to be because you are not allowed to hit a fly ball. You must let the ball bounce first. So, the smart player keeps all options open by staying out of that place.

If you hit a volley – a ball that has not bounced – you must be behind the kitchen line when you hit, and you must **remain behind the kitchen line even after you hit the ball**. For how long? There is no time limit. Long enough to demonstrate to others that you are solid on your feet with no faltering movement that will carry even one toe onto or across the kitchen line.

Faltering at the Kitchen Line

We know that you cannot hit the ball before it bounces if you are in the kitchen. You also cannot let your momentum from hitting a volley while behind the line carry you into the kitchen after you hit the ball.

If you are faltering near the kitchen line, trying to gain your footing but falling forward, your quick-thinking partner may be able to grab your shirt and pull you back before you cross the line. That's perfectly legal and that's what a good partner can do for you. The ideal pickleball shirt should include a handle on the back!

I have seen players try to avoid faltering across the kitchen line by bending forward and placing their paddle on the surface instead of a hand or foot. That doesn't cut it. No part of your body and nothing you are carrying or wearing may touch the kitchen. You can't even let your hat get blown off and land in the kitchen. One player got hit by a ball that knocked out a tooth which fell into the kitchen. The point was already over when the ball hit him, but the tooth in the kitchen was also a fault.

If your partner can't rescue you, about the only thing you can try is to cross the sideline before you violate the kitchen line so that when you do falter forward at least you are off the court. That's ok and it's great footwork.

The Third Shot Matters

What does it mean when people say they want to practice the 3rd shot drop? Why is it important?

As I've said ad infinitum, most points in pickleball are won at the kitchen line. That means the serve and return of serve are just introductory shots leading up to the important play. Whichever team gets to and controls the front part of the court first usually wins.

The receiving team starts out with a positioning advantage because 1 of the 2 players, that's 50% of the team, is already standing at the kitchen line, prime real estate. The receiver can join her partner up front as soon as she returns the serve. Meanwhile, both players on the serving team must stay back at their baseline until they see where the return of serve bounces.

The best way to take that positioning advantage away from your receiving team opponents when you are serving is to place that third shot softly into the kitchen. A short, soft shot means your opponent will have to take the ball on the bounce and hit upward. That takes away his chance of slamming it into your court and keeping you back at the baseline, or hitting at your feet as you move forward. The short shot **buys you time** to move forward and get in position for the volleying to come.

How to Handle Bangers

Bangers are those hard-hitting players who love the driving forehand shot and the big slams. Whether they picked this up from tennis or not, they rely on a longer back swing and take advantage of every ball we send their way that is above waist high. They like to play from the back of the court, and they keep you back as well.

What can you do when you play against the bangers? First, be sure you always have your **paddle up** and ready. You have no chance at all if your paddle is dropped in front of you or at your side. When you know you are about to get slammed, just hold your paddle out in a protective defense position and hope for the best.

Ease your grip. A paddle that is held loosely will absorb some of the impact of a hard-hit ball and slow the pace a bit. You can also use your body by bending your knees to absorb some of the impact.

Bangers hit a lot of balls that are going out, or that would be out if we **let them go**. So, be very conscious of speeding balls without a high arc. Instead of jumping up to snag a ball that might go out, bend over to tie your shoe and let the ball go.

Be aware of your court position. Get to the kitchen line or stay at the base. But don't get caught mid-court where you have little chance to deflect the ball or to return a controlled shot.

The above suggestions are only defensive. **You can't beat bangers at their own game**, so you must go on the offense by changing the game. That means hit soft serves and soft balls to bangers so they can't benefit from speed you put on the ball. Use the third shot drop. As soon as possible, get to the kitchen line and force a dinking rally that anyone might win.

Bad Habits Cost You Points

Bad habits are easy to acquire, but difficult to shed. If you can't reform, these behaviors will cost you points in every game.

Creeping Up Before the Return of Serve – Whether you or your partner is serving, you need to stay back at the baseline until the return of serve bounces. Many of us tend to creep forward. The opponents see this and hit a deep return. We get caught with the ball behind us or at our feet as we try to back up for a shot. Or, we lose our mind entirely and hit the return before it bounces. That's a rookie error.

Not Joining Partner at the Kitchen Line – When your team is receiving the serve, one of you starts at the kitchen line while the other stays back to receive.

This split in partners leaves a lot of court space open. If the receiver doesn't join the forward partner quickly, the opponents can easily place a ball behind the forward player out of reach of either one.

Stealing Partner's Shot - Taking a shot your partner was about to handle isn't going to win you friends. Some of us are more aggressive than others, maybe even ball hogs. And that's okay, if you communicate. Call the shot if you want to take it. The only thing worse than both of you going for the ball is neither of you going for it. Both situations can be avoided if you communicate with your partner. Speak up and speak often.

That's me reaching way too far with my backhand to steal my partner's forehand. Hope I called the shot at least.

Going for Tricky Serves – Trying to put extra juice on the ball during your serve is a risky play. Your team can't win if your serve isn't in. You not only risk blowing the shot, but your team loses the chance you were waiting for to score. So, start each game with a serve that's tame.

Impatience – The short game at the net is a game of patience. When you engage in a dinking rally, you need to wait for the right moment to hit a slam. The ball must be high enough for you to hit down on it rather than up and over. It can take a while, and patience is your friend. The player who can't stand to wait for the right ball usually faults.

Stopping Play Prematurely - A ball is not out of bounds until it touches the surface outside of the court. If a player yells "out" before the ball hits the ground, that "noise" is considered cross talk between players. It is not a valid call. It may prove to be right, or it may not. But don't stop playing. If you stop when someone yells prematurely, and the ball lands inbounds, you lose. The rules do not provide for do-overs.

Hitting Out Balls - If only those high fast balls weren't so tempting! Most of us love them. But we must learn to let them go. When you are near the kitchen line, and a ball is sailing at you shoulder high or more, it is probably going out. There is less than 15 feet of court space behind you. If you let it go, your team will win the rally. If you hit it anyway, there is a chance you will miss the shot. Even if you make a good shot, you have simply given your opponents another chance to get you.

Caught in the Kitchen – Stepping into the kitchen to return a short, soft dink is a good accomplishment. But if you don't move back behind the kitchen line right away, your nice effort will cost you the rally because your opponents will hit right at you.

What Was I Thinking?

Sometimes a game is going slowly. Maybe you are playing down, meaning your skills are superior to the other players on your court. Your opponents are targeting most of their shots at your weaker partner. **Your mind wanders:** what's for dinner; hmm, that's a nice top she's wearing; he needs to shave. Suddenly your team is falling behind in the score. You snooze, you lose.

To stay present in a less competitive game, pick something to work on. That will help you focus. Hit to each opponent's backhand only, or practice your 3rd shot drop. Count how many times a player hits a ball that would have gone out.

Turn your back to the net and count to three between points. Ask for a time out and have a drink of water. Regroup and get your mind back in the game.

Get Over It

Good players can lose points when they become agitated or mentally distracted. The biggest enemy of your mental game is self-flagellation. You miss a shot and you beat yourself up about it. Or you feel that the opponents called your shot out when you think it was good. You're stewing over it.

Maybe a hindrance occurs – an errant ball enters your court or a player from an adjoining court comes into your space. You should have stopped play but you didn't and now you are in a funk. Or someone stops play just when you were about to hit a winner and a replay occurs. Even a flying insect can be a valid distraction.

The best friend of your mental game is a short memory. Get over it right away. Look forward, not to the past.

On the other hand, if you know one of your opponents is still distracted by her last bad shot or a remark from her partner, she's the one you want to target.

This player looks like he's throwing a fit or maybe killing a spider. Was he caught in the kitchen?

Mentally distracted, he's the one you want to target.

The Stack Attack

The server must stand in a designated area: behind the baseline and between an imaginary extension of the center line and the sideline. But the server's partner may stand anywhere he wishes – on or off the court.

You may have noticed some players will stand on the same side of the court as their serving partner. This is known as "stacking." It is a strategy that advanced players sometimes use to take advantage of one player's particular strength – such as a powerful forehand – or to cover one player's weakness – such as a poor backhand. Stacking is most often seen when a team has one right hander and one left hander. It provides a way for the players to avoid weak positions on the court where both their backhands are in the center.

Of course, having both players on the same side would leave 1/2 of the court unattended – but only during the motion of the serve. As soon as the server connects with the ball, he crosses court and gets into the position that we would normally expect his partner to occupy. It's not for everyone, but it is legal.

Hmm, how does this work?

Stacking is confusing for your opponents, and sometimes for you as well.

A Word for the Bounce

Instructors and coaches tell us to take the pickleball in the air as a volley whenever you can, rather than bouncing it.

Maybe I'm just a contrarian because I see it differently. Here's why I sometimes favor the bounce. Taking the ball in the air is all about speed – giving your opponents **less time to react** or get into position. And that is a great advantage. But you also must be mighty quick to hit all volleys. And, you can only volley the higher shots that come to you, often reacting rather than plotting and controlling the delivery.

It's true that letting the ball bounce gives your opponents more time to get into position and anticipate your shot. But it also gives you more time to consider your options. What I have found is the longer I wait for the ball to bounce, the more entrenched the opponents get in their positions waiting for the action. If I am patient and can disguise my return shot, I will hit a well-placed winner. Since I am not much of a slammer, I find more finesse opportunities if I let the ball bounce. To each her own. . .

Are you a Ball Chaser?

Some players remind me of dogs during play time. They seem to be happy chasing balls. And the younger ones, the puppies, are remarkably quick and agile. They can get to some very difficult shots, back up their partners, and sometimes still get back in place for the next volley.

Those of us without young legs need to learn to anticipate the ball better. The sooner you can read where your opponent is likely to hit, the better you can react.

It takes practice and experience. Always watch the ball, even if you are not actively in the shot. Watch before your opponent strikes the ball; what is the angle of his paddle? The face of the paddle, the direction of the feet and the position of the leading shoulder are all clues to where the ball is coming on your court. And, an opponent's open paddle face generally produces spin on the ball.

Pickleball is a very fast game. Every second you gain in anticipation will pay off.

Body Language

You don't have to be a mind reader in pickleball. Studying your opponent's body language can give you great clues about the shots coming your way. Start with the head and eyes. Most players signal where they want the ball to go by looking in that direction. A player who knows how to shift weight and follow through on shots will also turn a leading shoulder in the direction of her target.

How quickly does your opponent move between points? A slow shuffle can mean the poor guy is getting worn out, or just getting frustrated by unforced errors. That's the opponent you should target.

Watch for dropped paddles. When a player consistently lets her paddle drop below the waist or at the side, try hitting straight at her middle girth. You will jam her, and she can't get her paddle up in time.

You can often spy your opponent shifting his weight from one side to another. He's signaling that he expects your ball to come on that side of his reach. So of course, you surprise him by hitting to his other side.

She must have let her paddle drop and now she's trying to get out of a jam.

Body language is a two-way communication. You can convey a lot of disinformation very deliberately if you wish. Stand tall with paddle raised while waiting for your partner to receive a serve. It subtly distracts the server. Shuffle slightly back and forth creating a moving target. Look in one direction then skillfully hit an angled shot in another direction. It's not that difficult, you can do it.

My favorite offensive body language is conveying a message with your face. Some players wear a very fierce look, especially when they are at the kitchen line about to hit. It can seem intimidating and it works. A friend of mine once said, "my face, I don't mind it for I am behind it; the other guy gets the fright."

Double Hit, Carry & Other Tricks

Part of the fun of pickleball is things you can get away with. The rules makers were pretty understanding!

At times the ball seems to stick to your paddle or hesitates before deciding where to go. **The ball can be hit twice or "carried,"** as long as this occurs during one continuous single direction stroke. But, it must be accidental, not deliberate, so you can't make this part of your strategy.

It's also **okay if the ball hits your fingers or hand**, as long as it's your paddle hand and below the wrist. If your skin takes the hit, it is still a good shot even if the ball missed your paddle entirely.

It's okay to **switch hands** at any time during play. Sometimes it's a last resort effort to reach a wide shot. I've seen players who try this get pretty good at it.

It's also okay to make **two-handed shots**, though you probably need small hands since the paddle handle isn't very long. If you have two hands on the paddle, the ball may hit either hand below the wrist and it's still good. A two-for-one advantage.

Sometimes a player will **swing and miss** the ball entirely. This isn't baseball so that is not an error, although it will become a fault if the player's partner doesn't back him up and get that shot. A fast player can swing and miss a volley but recover quickly enough to take another swing at the ball, thanks to the bounce. It happens.

Look Ma, No Hands

Backspin is a beautiful thing. It confuses your opponents and makes you seem like a pro. It is amazing. But more often than you can imagine, a ball is hit into the opponents' kitchen with so much backspin that it actually pops back onto your side of the net before either of the opponents touches it.

Your opponents can't take credit for that hands-free return. It is a fault against them because they weren't fast enough to hit the ball before it returned to you by itself.

I Get Around

If a ball hits the net post, it is a fault. But if a ball hits the net or the top net wire that secures the net to the post, and lands in bounds, it remains in play.

However, the ball may not pass through the open area between the net and the net post.

Once in a while, you get a chance to dazzle the opponents when their shot pulls you wide. You are permitted to return a ball around the **outside of the net post**. It doesn't have to go over the net, nor does it have to be as high as the net. It just has to land in the opponents' court. And you must do this without moving onto the opponent's side of the court.

This player was pulled wide and is preparing to return the ball around the post.

It's Touchy

Some of us are tactile so beware the net. You **may not touch the net**, ever, when the ball is in play. Think of it as barbed wire.

Be careful not to hit the net or the net system (posts and wires) with your paddle or with anything you are wearing or carrying. whether it is due to a follow through when striking the ball, or just a smack to express frustration.

Don't reach across the net to strike a ball. That's not okay. Wait for the ball to cross the plane of the net (an imaginary extension of the net upwards into the sky.) It's okay if you follow through your shot by reaching over the net.

So what can you touch? Well, you can touch yourself, touch the back fence, or the netting separating courts. You could touch your partner or a spectator but do so at your own risk!

Oops, How Did I Hit That?

Sometimes we need an assist, but the only thing your ball is permitted to hit on its way into the opponents' court is the net. That's because the net is mostly within the boundary lines of the court and is considered part of the court. Other than let serves, a ball that hits the net is good, still in play.

The net posts, on the other hand, are placed outside of the court boundary lines. If you hit the net post, it is a fault against you, even if the ball ricochets into the opponents' court. Likewise, if you hit a fence, a bench or any other permanent object, it is a fault against you, and time for an eye exam. But, if the ball you hit bounces into the opponent's court, and then hits a net post or any permanent object before anyone else hits it, you win the rally! Maybe you can find a way to practice that!

You Wear the Stripes

We don't have referees at drop-in pickleball, so you wear the stripes. That means you must make the call when a ball is out on your side of the court. An out call is a fault against your opponents. Some players make these calls gleefully, others are very reluctant to call anything out. But it is your responsibility, so buck up.

The perimeter lines are part of the court. A ball that lands on a line is good. A ball that lands entirely outside of the lines is out.

Call "out" balls clearly and promptly as you see them. You or your partner may call a ball out **on your side of the net only**. If neither of you saw the ball land, then it is presumed good. If the ball was too close to call, then it is presumed good. If you call it out and your partner disagrees with your call, the ball is presumed good. Pro and social players play close balls rather than calling them out. It's the best thing to do. You should be able to win a game with good shots, not close calls.

If you call the ball on your side of the court "out" and the opponents say that it looked good, the ball is still out. End of story. **It's not their call**. The opponents don't get a say in the call on your side of the net unless you ask them. Sometimes an opponent may have a better view of a sideline and you would like to ask what the opponent saw. If you do ask, you must agree with whatever the opponent says.

How far does your good sportsmanship go? If you hit a ball that you see lands wide, yet your opponents don't call it out, do you turn yourself in, so to speak? You are permitted to make a call against yourself, and many players do. That is the only way you can reverse your opponent's call – or in this case a non-call.

When you make line calls, don't be equivocal, just do your best. How would you like to hear your dentist say "I think that was the right tooth," or, have your banker say "that check to the IRS might have bounced?"

"I think it was long" or "that might be wide" doesn't cut it. If you believe a shot is out, say it loudly, clearly, and with conviction. **Shout it "OUT."** You don't have to explain or justify your call.

The rules do not provide for do-overs because players can't agree on a line call. Any doubt, then the ball was good. Good sportsmanship is just as important as good playing skills.

Don't stop playing because you think a ball is going out. It's ok to return a ball after it has bounced out of bounds. The ball is still out if you or your partner call it after you return it. Play stops with the call. Just make the call before the opponents have another shot back to you.

Saying It Doesn't Make It So

A ball is **not out of bounds until it lands** outside of the court. If a player yells "out" before the ball hits the ground, it is **not a valid call** whether that was the intention or not. It may prove to be right, or it may not. But don't stop playing. If you stop when someone yells prematurely, and the ball lands inbounds, you lose. The rules do not provide for do-overs.

If you catch a ball that was obviously going out of bounds before it hits the ground, you lose. It is a fault against you, even if you were standing well outside the court lines when you caught it. Like I said, a ball is not out until it hits the ground outside of the court, so if you catch it you prevent it from landing.

Maybe there is a practical exception. I've seen balls hit so far out they land in an adjacent tree or on top of a shed or shade awning and never come down. I think we would have to say it is out, wouldn't we?

Hitting it Doesn't Change the Call

It's okay to return a ball that touched out of bounds and then call it out after you hit it. **Just because you hit the ball does not make it is good,** nor does it prevent a delayed line call. In fact, you should not stop playing because you think a ball is going to be out. Play it through, then make the call. But make the call before the opponents send it back again.

If someone stopped playing because they thought a ball was going out, but it did not get called out, too bad, it was good.

Who Calls Kitchen Violations?

A kitchen violation occurs when a player hits a volley while the player, or anything the player is holding or wearing, touches the kitchen area or the kitchen line. "Hitting a volley" includes the back swing, the follow through, and the momentum from the action.

Any player on either team who sees a kitchen violation may, and should, call it. Under a new (2020) rule, any doubt or disagreement about the kitchen call will result in a replay.

Any player on either team may also call a let ball during the serve, or a service foot fault.

Correcting the Score

It seems that pickleball rallies get pretty intense because players often lose track of the score. Disputes occur. How do you protest? Well, there's a rule for that.

Any player can stop play **before the return of serve** to ask for a correction of the score. If the wrong score was called, the server will call the correct score and play resumes with no penalties. BUT, if there was no error in the score that was called, the player who stopped the game has committed a fault. Also, it is a fault against you if you stop play **after the return of serve** to dispute the score, regardless whether the score called was right or not.

But really, if someone tried to enforce this in social play, he would be booed off the court.

Bottom line: **don't let a score call distract you**. Play it safe and wait until after play stops to discuss - and sometimes negotiate – the correct score.

Getting Away with It

Sometimes you get away with things. But in doubles play there is usually someone watching. Here are many of the things you just shouldn't do, even among friends. Violations are faults against you.

1. Cross the baseline before your serve leaves your paddle.
2. Serve when it is your partner's turn. Or, receive a serve when it isn't your turn.
3. Serve before the score is called.
4. Hit the return of serve before it bounces.
5. Touch the net when the ball is in play.
6. Touch any part of the kitchen, including the line, while hitting a volley. Stumble on or across the kitchen line after hitting your volley from behind the line.
7. Catch a ball in play before it hits the ground.
8. Continue playing a point after the ball hits you.

Do-Overs

There are very few times when you get a "do-over" in pickleball.

The most common second chances are when you hit a let serve, or when play is stopped because an errant ball or an over-zealous player from another court enters your court, interfering with play. You must also re-serve if you serve before the receiver is ready. That's pretty much it.

Notice, there is nothing about re-doing a point because no one saw whether the ball was in or out, or because there was a difference of opinion on that matter. Whenever no one sees the ball land, or two people see it differently, the ball is considered good, and do-overs are neither legal nor appropriate.

Net Bars That Get in the Way

The stabilizing bar along the lower part of collapsible nets on many courts can cause some problems. Here is what the latest rules say:

1. If the ball hits the horizontal bar before going over the net, it is a fault against you.
2. If your ball goes over the net and then hits the horizontal bar, or gets caught between the net and the horizontal bar before touching the opponents' court, it is a do-over and must be replayed, unless this happens on the serve, which would be a fault.

What About Those Side Arm Serves?

You've heard the rules: serve must be underhanded; paddle must strike ball at or below the waist; highest part of paddle head must be below or even with the wrist when it strikes the ball; arm must be moving in an upward arc. So, are those side arm serves legal?

Well, some are, and some aren't. In some cases only an experienced referee with a discerning eye can see the distinction. You may get away with the sidearm in social play, though if other players see you crossing the edge on your serve, they may wonder about your line calls and other aspects of your game.

Why push your luck? It's nice to score an ace, but pickleball isn't about serving. It's about dinking and placement and all the smart moves that come after the two-bounce rule is satisfied.

Ready or Not?

There are two ways a receiver may signal to a server that he is not ready. Either raise one hand above your head or turn your back to the server. I suppose if I see you sit down on the ground, or walk off the court, or yell "wait", I would get that you are not ready.

Your not-ready signal must be given before the server begins the service motion. Once in motion, the receiver cannot become "not ready". The only thing that can stop the serve is legitimate interference such as an errant ball entering your court, or a clueless person walking onto your court.

When is Exuberance Illegal?

I've stressed the importance of communicating with your partner. You might call shots, yell warnings about balls that are likely going out, call your partner to switch positions, or warn your partner when you see a ball with spin coming his way. All of that is generally okay. But, yelling when an opponent is about to strike the ball might be considered an illegal distraction. And you won't get away with yelling something that is "not common to the game," like "your mama wears combat boots" or whatever they say nowadays.

Some players can sleep through a thunderstorm and others wake to a bird call. Some pickleball players don't hear well; some are too focused to be bothered by your talk. It's all in the ear of the individual. But to be safe from accusations of interference, you might want to use your indoor voice and stick to pickleball language.

Time's Up

The clock matters only a couple times in pickleball. Of course, in social play time flies when we are having fun and we don't click the stopwatch.

When all players are in place, and the score has been called, the server is permitted 10 seconds to serve the ball. If you can't manage that, it's a fault against you. So, don't overthink it.

During a typical game, each team is allowed two timeouts of up to one minute each. Some players use this time to hydrate and regroup. Others answer their phones.

Medical time outs are more generous. An injured player may take up to 15 minutes to recover, although we know the second someone limps off one of our courts, an anxious bystander will step in. If you do get injured, try to show some blood. You are permitted a time out for as long as it takes to stop the bleeding!

Forget about official timeouts. When you are thirsty or feeling faint, stop between points to take a drink. You should have done that sooner. Need to massage a cramp, just take the time to do it. Gonna sneeze? Go for it. No one will clock you during drop-in play times.

Are You Kidding Me?

Here are some actual provisions from the official rule book that I won't cover. But you have to wonder what the rule makers saw that made them create these regulations.

"*A player must be in possession of the paddle when it makes contact with the ball.*" Are you kidding me? Did someone try to return a lob shot by throwing his paddle up in the air? If you aren't in possession of your paddle, maybe your paddle is possessed!

"*A player shall not use or carry more than one paddle while playing.*" I guess that keeps it fair for all those players who aren't ambidextrous.

"*You are not permitted to add moving parts or springs to your paddle*". Hmm, there goes my Science Fair project.

"*A player may be required to change garments that are inappropriate.*" This is to avoid unnecessary distractions. I watched a 20-something fit young man playing shirtless and shoeless on our courts last summer. No clothes is more distracting than inappropriate ones.

"*Any writing on apparel or paddles must be in good taste.*" Well, the game started in the 60's. Make love, not war was the least offensive of the graphics I remember.

"*If the ball bounces into a receiver's court with enough backspin...to return back over the net, a player may reach under the net to return the ball*" but of course can't touch the net. What the . . .? This is pickleball, not limbo. How would I ever be able to do that??

"If a player is injured during a game, the rally must continue to conclusion before play is stopped." Ha, you thought pickleball was a social game. . .it's a blood sport! Try not to step on your partner if he is on the ground writhing from pain while you finish the point.

"If an injury is self-inflicted, the player is charged with a technical warning or foul." Geez, did someone really try to commit hari kari over a bad shot?

What's the Limit Quiz?

How many times can you serve a let ball and get another chance to serve it?

How high can the score go in a pickleball game?

How many toes can cross the kitchen line before it is considered a fault?

How high is a pickleball net in the middle? How high at the ends?

How large can a pickleball paddle be (width + length of paddle including handle)?

How many players does it take to remember the score?

How many times can one person serve in a row?

How many people can have fun playing pickleball at once on one tennis court?

Answers:

As many times as it takes to get it right.

As high as you can count or until the game is called for darkness.

Only one toe, or any part of your shoe.

34 inches middle, 36 inches ends.

24 inches.

Sounds like a trick question.

12 – assumes the opponents collect 10 points before your team gets a chance to serve. You take over and if you are good, and lucky, you could serve 12 times in a row and win by the required 2 points. Of course, a person could serve all day if he keeps hitting let balls.

16 players plus all the cheerleaders on the sidelines.

Pickleball Survivor Guide

I'm not much for reality tv shows, but I make an exception for Survivor. Are you a fan? There have been 41 seasons of Survivor, and it's still going, so I'm not the only one who is hooked. The show's motto is:

Outwit, Outplay, Outlast. That strikes me as a perfect description of winning at pickleball.

<u>Outwit</u> is the strategic part of the game. This is where you place shots for winners, set up shots for your partner to hit a winner, size up the competition and take advantage of their apparent weaknesses. Good strategy involves getting into position on the court so you can play offensively rather than defensively.

<u>Outplay</u> is avoiding unforced errors. If you make a mistake when your team is serving, you lose a chance to score. If you err when your opponents are serving, you just gave them a point. With luck, you can recover from some errors like hitting a high ball to your opponents, but there is no recovery from errors like hitting into the net.

<u>Outlast</u> is my favorite part of the game, patience. Learn to just keep a ball in play and bide your time until the right opportunity opens up. Then carpe diem, seize it. The players who can't wait for the right moment usually make mistakes.

In Survivor the winner gets a million bucks while all the losers get voted off the island. In pickleball the Survivor gets bragging rights, and the losers have to leave the court until the next game.

PART 4: PLAYING WELL, STAYING WELL

<u>It's Elemental</u>

Many basics can affect your play. If you want to win games, leave your troubles at home. Clear your head and focus on the challenges at hand. No one needs an extra distraction.

Keep a good level of overall fitness. Cross training is helpful for most sports. Pickleball challenges your hand/eye coordination, flexibility, and core muscle strength more than many sports.

Hydrate before, during and after play. Can't stress this enough. A dry body is brittle and susceptible to injuries and ailments.

Stretch before playing – from head and neck to toes. Warm up so your muscles are primed, and your eyes are focused on the ball. Bounce on those knees to get them ready. A body that is warmed is like tenderized meat – supple and able to take new forms.

Consider the day and how the elements will affect your game. What way is the wind blowing and how steady is it? How high is the sun and where are the longest shadows? When you are on the good side of these natural elements, use them to your advantage and accumulate some points before the game is half over and your opponents demand you change sides for the duration of the game.

Every day is different. Sometimes you can do no wrong and every net ball falls in your favor. Other days your money shots fail you and you can't get anything going. Even pros have slumps. It will come back. And remember, it's only a game.

Get Advice, Use it or Not

I can't tell you how many ski lessons I've had over the years to conquer the moguls. Finally, one instructor in Killington talked about knees being like bedsprings. That image did it for me. Eureka, let it snow!

Most social players are interested in getting better while enjoying the game. Ask a player you admire for some tips. Even unsolicited advice can have value. You don't have to follow the advice you are given but if it makes sense to you, try it. Always thank the other player whether you like what he says or not.

And, of course, there is a whole world of clinics, coaches and lessons you can explore if you wish to make a serious commitment.

If you are the stronger player on your team, offer a tip at the end of a game. Just one thing at a time. But consider your bedside – or net side - manner. There are even kind ways to tell a floundering player that she should take up croquet instead.

Where There's a Will, There's a Drill

Practice makes perfect, or at least better. If you want to improve your skills, you need to put time into practice drills. Working on your overall fitness helps too, but that's another book.

<u>Alone? Don't Groan</u> – You don't need a practice partner to work on your serve. Just go to the courts at an off time, take a basket of balls, and practice serving from the right and left sides of a court. Your first goal is to land safe serves 90% of the time. Next, work at targeting your serve to land at your opponents' feet and backhand side. Use a hula hoop or make a circle out of string and place it where you want your serves to land. How many hit your target? When you feel good about that, use a smaller circle or a basket as the target.

The other variable to practice is pace. Moderate or fast serves can be alternated with slow balls or high serves.

You can also practice hand/eye coordination and tracking the ball when you are alone. You don't even need to be at a court. Just hit the ball up in the air with your paddle. Always watch the ball as you keep hitting it without letting it bounce. Count the hits. Can you get to 100 times? If so, now hit the ball 100 times without moving your feet. This requires a bit more control. Need an extra challenge? Alternate which side of the paddle face you use to hit the ball each time, like forehand and backhand movements. Or try hitting off the edge.

<u>Partner Drills</u> – If you find a practice partner who is interested in working with you to get better, congratulations. You two can go places. Making time to execute drills really pays off.

Pick one thing to practice each time, and your partner will feed you balls. You can create repetitive drills for dinking, cross-court dinking, forehand and backhand ground strokes, serve and return of serve, third shot soft drops. Practice softening fast shots as well.

Repetitive drills will give you muscle memory and faster reaction times when the shots are required in live play. Execution will become more automatic and predictable.

Sidelined or Rained Out

Here are some things you can do to stay in the game when you are sidelined by an injury or when the weather has cancelled play.

1. Watch some training videos or tournament play. Google to find a number of good sites.
2. Practice keeping a spring in your knees. Bounce around the house, reaching to gently swipe at small items on the floor like the cat, or a crumbled sheet of paper. Keeping knees flexible saves your back and helps prevent falls. (You might want to turn off your Alexa Show or other video before you do this!)
3. Strengthen your core muscles with regular sit-up exercises. A strong core protects your back and helps control balance. It's your power center.
4. Bounce a ball on your paddle, keeping your eye on the ball the whole time. One of those kid's toy paddles with a rubber ball attached on an elastic string is a great eye trainer.
5. Clean your paddle. Wipe with a damp cloth and a bit of gentle dish detergent. Dry with a soft cloth. Check the grip. While you are at it, check the treads on your shoes. Neither your grip nor your shoes should be slippery.
6. Reread this book while you practice hydrating.

Am I Good or What?

After playing for a while, you become aware of some peoples' obsession with their rating. We used to be happy in college with some pass/fail scores. Now everyone wants to be a 3.5 or better. Official ratings rank from 1.0 (Beginner) to 5.5+ (I Never Lose.)

When you play in a sanctioned tournament you will earn an official rating that will be tracked for future use. You may also apply for an official rating by submitting a skill self-assessment, attested to by certain USAPA agents familiar with your playing skills, along with a promise to turn over your first born. That last requirement may have been overturned in the courts. But you get the idea.

Your tennis rating does not transfer to pickleball. Just because you can ride a pony doesn't mean you can handle a racehorse.

If you really want to pursue a rating, check out the process at: https://www.usapa.org/player-skill-rating-definitions/

Tsk, Tsk, Don't Take the Risk

Always stop play when an errant ball or an out of control player from an adjoining court enters your space. Doesn't matter whether you were about to win or lose the point. Safety first. Even pesky flying insects count as a legitimate hindrance.

Play It Safe in the Sun

Now that you are hooked on pickleball, you will be outdoors exposed to the sun more often. Getting your vitamin D is good, but burnt skin and wrinkles are not. Sunscreen and sun protective clothing are important. Did you know that one in five of us will develop skin cancer? It is more prevalent than breast, prostate, lung and colon cancers **combined!** And some forms of skin cancer are deadly.

Protection is so easy: use sunscreen every day, wear a hat, cover your arms and chest with UV protective clothing that is lightweight for all seasons. Don't be fooled if the sun hides behind clouds some days. It still has a powerful impact on you.

People with nice hair might like to show it off and leave the hat at home. That vanity could be fatal. Sun damage from UV rays is cumulative and irreversible. We are living longer, staying active outdoors for many years, and some of us live in sunny or high-altitude climates. It all adds up.

No Fear, Wear Safety Gear

Protecting your eyes from injury is also critical. You should always wear some type of **eye protection**. Sunglasses are good. If you don't like them, get a pair of athletic eye guards. A hat with a big brim offers some eye protection but glasses are better. I saw one spectator take a paddle to the face when she was on the sidelines. She was talking on her phone and wandered too close to the action while a competitive player on the adjacent court took a big backswing. Her sunglasses saved her, though I don't think she came back the next day.

Cumulative exposure to sun damages eyes as well as skin. Besides protecting from injury, sunglasses protect eyes from UV rays that can cause cataracts, and from blue light rays that can lead to macular degeneration.

Did you know, when you wear sunglasses in the daytime your eyes are able to adjust more easily to darkness, such as driving at night. Sunglasses also make vision more comfortable without awkward squinting. Squinting encourages wrinkles around the eyes. Who needs that?!

People with blue eyes are most susceptible to sun damage, but everyone should be cautious. If the health benefits don't persuade you, sunglasses also

disguise your pickleball shots! Opponents can't see where you are looking to place your return.

You probably don't need a breastplate, athletic cup or helmet for further protection playing pickleball, but **no one is so good at pickleball they never make an errant shot.** Players have been hit by the ball in the chest, face, hands, legs and private parts, usually by an opponent, sometimes by their own partner, and occasionally self-inflicted. Bruises and pride heal. Just keep those eyes covered.

Don't Blow a Tire

Check your shoe treads regularly. Rubber loses elasticity in dry climates, and all the starting and stopping movement in pickleball wears down the treads on your shoes faster than other sports. You wouldn't drive your car with bald tires. Don't expose yourself to falls with slippery shoes.

I have seen the sole on one player's worn shoes come apart like an old retread tire. He managed not to fall, but he did have a fall from grace. Examine your favorite shoes regularly. I know, they're comfortable because you've broken them in so well, but they won't last forever. **Worn shoes = falls.**

The sole is coming apart, a disaster in the making.

A spritz of Lysol after each play session helps keep your shoes fresh inside while the treads are still good. I learned that from my germaphobe husband.

Falling for Pickleball

A good thing about pickleball is that it is fun at all skill and fitness levels. The problem with pickleball is that it is fun at all skill and fitness levels. Some athletically challenged people come out to play. Falls do occur on the courts. Even fit players can take a tumble, especially when they play hard and put winning ahead of whining.

Falling head over heels is okay for romance, but in pickleball you want to **rock and roll**. When falling, you need to protect your head above all else. Some players have replacement body parts – knees, shoulders, hips. One of our players has a prosthetic leg. But I have never seen a replacement head.

To protect the only head you will ever have, curl into a fetal position with your hands protecting your head and **roll, roll, roll with the fall.** Just like the stunt men and women do in the action movies. You have a lot of padding, muscle and fat, in your lower body. Let it take the brunt of the fall while you curl and roll to protect your head. Trying to stop a fall by holding out your arms puts you at risk for a broken wrist or shoulder injury and leaves your skull and what's inside exposed.

You should never back up during play. There is a reason we have eyes in the front only. That is the direction our bodies are meant to move. Backing up, especially while looking up, changes your center of gravity and leads to the worst kind of falls. If you must chase a lob shot, pivot 180 degrees and move to the baseline hoping to reach the shot even if you execute a blind return. Or pivot 90 degrees and sidestep to the back of the court.

Don't play on wet courts. If it rains, take the day off, get some indoor exercise – like bowling, gin rummy or making babies. In the fall when the courts have seasonal debris – leaves, pine needles, etc – take the time to sweep the slippery rubble aside. Injuries from falls can take a long time to heal completely, and no one wants to be sidelined.

The Language of Pickleball

A game as fast as pickleball requires an abbreviated language to communicate. New players learn that the "non-volley zone", the first 7 feet on each side of the net, is called the "kitchen". A "dink" is a shot intended to land in the opponents' kitchen. Yelling "no" to your partner is short for "let it go" which is short for "I think it's going to be out so don't hit it." "Ball" means "there is a stray ball on or approaching our court and we need to stop play before someone gets hurt."

"Good shot" to your opponent means "how did I miss that? I better get with it." "Nice try" to your partner, 3 times in a row, means "this guy stinks, I need a new partner." "#$!!" means "how did I blow that shot?" "Switch" means "I know you can't get that lob, so I'm running behind you to hit it. You need to move across to cover the other side of the court."

"Back" means the opponents are going to take that high shot we gave them and slam it back at us. We have a better chance of defending if we move back now."

"Ballet" can be short for a score of 2-2-2 (tutus). Or, sometimes "trains" means 2-2-2 (choo, choo, choo.) "Sale" can mean a score of 2-4-1.

"I need to sit one out" can mean you need a break, or it might mean you really don't want to play in the next game with those players. "Who served that?" often means that you forgot it was you who served. "Bagel" means one team has 0 points. "Happy birthday" means "I know I just gave you a gift by hitting the ball that would have gone out. You're lucky." "Sorry" to your opponent when you hit a winner that taps the top of the net and rolls down on the opponents' side of the court means "lucky me, ha ha."

However you abbreviate it, pb, pball, and pickling all mean a great way to get exercise and have fun.

Pickleball Mantras

These simple sayings can help you focus on winning strategies while you play. So, keep these tips on your lips.

Eye on the ball says it all.

Your team can't win if your serve isn't in.

Serve it tame to start the game.

Talk more, improve your score.

Hit it low, steal the show.

Hit in-between, split the team.

Keep your partner near your heart,
never get too far apart.

Hit at the feet, you will defeat.

Whattya say? Just keep it in play.

Bend at the knees, please.

You git what you hit.

Hit at the toes, not the nose.

Play it smart, hit where they aren't.

When in doubt, don't call it out.

Don't think, just dink.

Have Paddle Will Travel

It's easy to pack your paddle in carry-on luggage when you travel. Check the USAPA website to find places to play. Or lead a grass roots effort to fabricate a temporary court in an unlikely place like a cruise ship or a wide driveway. Necessity is the mother of invention. https://www.places2play.org/

Relishing the Sport

By now you should be pickled, in the best of ways. This sport is like a drug: it gets you high, it relaxes your inhibitions, makes you giddy with laughter, cures what ails you, and becomes addictive. Pass it around!

Feedback is welcome. I would love to hear from you. Contact me at: inclinepickleball@gmail.com

If you enjoyed this book, please leave a brief review on amazon.com.

Other books by Beverly Keil:

Diary of a Dumpster Pup – saving the life of an abandoned newborn puppy.

Sleepless in New Orleans – come along on a hurricane animal rescue mission.

Books by Douglas Keil:

Killdeer – A young attorney may be in over her head when she enters the high security SuperMax prison to confront the FBI's notorious Soviet spy and uncover the secret he holds.

The Girl in the Freezer – Can a clever reporter outwit a wealthy secret society of genetic scientists?

Deadline – Can an absent father protect his genius daughter from her destiny?

BarCats – a naive young man is caught in the crosshairs of the Feds and the Mafia after falling for the Don's niece.

Dear Dad – true story of an adolescent's journey through adversity; emotional, inspiring and humorous.

Made in the USA
Middletown, DE
10 December 2020